Brandon Pithouse
**Recollections of the
Durham Coalfield**

Brandon Pithouse
**Recollections of the
Durham Coalfield**
John Seed

Smokestack Books
1 Lake Terrace, Grewelthorpe, Ripon HG4 3BU
e-mail: info@smokestack-books.co.uk
www.smokestack-books.co.uk

ISBN 978-0-9934547-0-7

Smokestack Books is
represented by Inpress Ltd

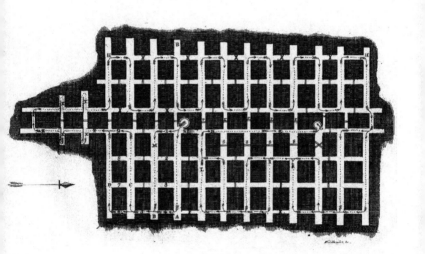

Grey fields old

Enclosures bounded thorn

Scattered oak ash

Shafts of light from above

Wintry landscape

Or seascape what was

Not there what was

Crunch of icy tyre-tracks underfoot

Daylight already old

Looking beyond the visible beyond

Brandon Pithouse

Ragpath Drift

———————————

in short breeches

low shoes and

cotton skull-cap

swinging his

5 lb pick while

sweat runs white

down black cheeks

always in peril

of gas or

fall of stone

or sudden flood or

whoever he is

1

grandmother sent me a good door-string
six farthing candles for bait
some of her best currant bread

bait poke over my shoulder
candle-box in my pocket through darkness
along the black wagon-way up

past the pit-pond by the pick shop to the pit-heap
clanking of engines creaking pulleys overhead
hoarse voices of men calling answering

————————

at the pit's-mouth banksman calling down the shaft
hewers coming up two by two or three by six or
anyhow as the rope brought them

men emptying corves
boys wailing rough coals
discarding stones and slates
long line of sheds the screens

————————

Low Main seam (coal 20 inches thick) – 57ft. from the surface
Hutton seam (coal 32 inches thick) – 157ft. from the surface
Harvey seam (coal 24 inches thick) – 312ft. from the surface
Busty seam (coal 48 inches thick) – 418ft. from the surface
Brockwell seam (coal 34 inches thick) – 522ft. from the surface

one minute to descend by cage
five hundred and thirty seven concrete steps to the Busty
ten minutes carrying an eight-pound electric lamp tokens shot
powder sharp picks

———————————

Nigh-hand gannen
parallel passages called boards
four yards wide eight yards asunder
connected by headways
smaller passages at right angles twenty yards apart
leaving strong pillars of coal to support the roof

headways and boards at right lines through the whole extent of
the mine

seams of coal generally extend a great way
rising or falling or horizontal
workings branch out from one another
an immense number of dark passages

2

'Left as a bare frame, or enclosed in cladding, the winding tower gave the pit its identity; along the coast, by day or night (when they were lit up) they formed sure landmarks to boats at sea.'

(Bill Griffiths)

Miners are hewers

stone-sinkers putters enginemen timber-drawers shot-firers
waste-men horse-keepers and drivers   underground …

And banksmen masons fitters joiners sawyers blacksmiths
boilersmiths horse-shoers plumbers saddlers painters
electricians lamp-repairers platelayers smiths' strikers winding
enginemen engine drivers hauliers ostlers carters
rolleywaymen screen and washery engineers stokers
patternmakers rope splicers ashmen boiler cleaners shunters
power-house men topmen in charge of signals …   And their
wives and daughters and mothers and sisters and

————————————

You walk into any pit house ten o' clock at night
find the same thing
red hot fire
a tired-looking woman
heavy damp clothes hanging up
all over the place

————————————

shafts and drifts
heapstead hoppers
workshops stables
long batteries of coke-ovens
hiss and whistle of steam
engines smoke from furnace chimneys
gas from slaked ovens bells
clanging the winding signals
clanking coal trucks bumped shunting
railway sidings 400 yards from the pit
metal-capped boots
going down the street lanterns on caps thumbs tucked into
string belts we were always aware of the shifts as
the buzzer went the sound was
continuous when someone
was killed and all the miners came out of the
pit when the man died or the colliery closed or
they were dismissed the family had to leave the house
and move on   people often moved on

————————————

Bromdun Bramdom Brampdon Brandon
1871: 1926 inhabitants 10 streets 281 houses

'miserable huts' for families one small room
ladder to the unceiled attic

floors of square quarls
iron boiler one side of the fireplace
round oven the other

still collecting water from rain barrels from springs in the fields
scores of bee-hive coke ovens south of the pit
Irish housed in Railway and South Streets 'Little Ireland'

———————————

two-up two-down cottages
each brick stamped with the name of the colliery company

cold water tap in the pantry
backyard the tin bath

wood back gate the goal
and next to the coalhouse the ash-pit

lav ash-midden netty
whitewashed walls and tied with string

squares of newspaper or occasionally
soft paper wrappings from oranges

———————————

Wash day the devil's birthday
living room reeking with steam
dodging damp vests drawers shirts sheets pillow-cases
drying pegged out across the
front of the fire place
dim light of an oil-lamp or candle

---

telling time by the colliery buzzer
to the women at home to
tell them their men were coming home
start setting the table

Roddymoor
hewer drilled a hole
put a pellet of powder into it
another pellet on the floor
by a lighted candle he knocked
the candle over the powder exploded

Some of them never used to wash their back

weaken their back if they took the dirt off

a right concern
gettin the water ready and filled the bath

and the clothes dadded and cleaned and
hung on them
at the front of the houses

———————————

When a neighbour's husband
was in night shift
we were told
not to play round the doors.

———————————

sinkers at Blackhall in 1909
for their wives and families

built huts out of
packing cases on the beach banks

at Blackhall Rocks there were still
families of pitmen in the 1930s

Irish immigrants tin miners
from Cornwall among them

living in huts on the beach
or caves

———————

Going in-bye to his work
some men in front of him
got into a refuge hole to
let a set of tubs pass
but he went on
mind elsewhere
hit
and died the same day

———————

Coalminers as % of occupied males in County Durham

1841	16.1
1851	21.1
1861	20.8
1871	17.1
1881	24.3
1891	25.0
1901	26.0
1911	33.4

3

Dick Morris

It was the custom among miners for them

to take their sons with them

in the school holidays

and I was down

Oh I should think

a dozen times

with me dad

in the school holidays

just to see

was to get you acclimatised

the inevitable way of life

———————————

William Cowburn

You knew
long before you left school
that's where you were going when you left school that was
what you were

born for really to go down the pit

I should never been a pitman
in them days like
lots of liked the thought of going down
them getting a pony to drive
bit of attraction

but then I'm not frightened to admit
I was terrified when I went down the pit
I think I cried all the first shift

place was infested with rats
used to come out in swarms
come right to your feet
after the ponies' corn

———————————

I asked to go into the pit
to get away from school

I would go to school now
if I could be allowed

———————

In the summer we go down at five.
In winter at three and up between three and four.
We come up in summer two or three in the afternoon.

Summer time when the work is not hard after the pit we play marbles and try to catch quoits and cricket and striking a ball against the wall.
Some boys go and fish eels in the river.
In winter time the hours are harder and when we come home we are fit enough to go to bed.

———————

overman, back-overman and ten deputies clearing away a fall of side-stone in the morning the stone is a mild blue with a very close grain affected by variations in the temperature and the weather was hot

when there was a second fall
displacing two baulks and a prop the roof fell in
killing three deputies injuring two

———————

left school Monday

started work down the pit

Tuesday I was 14

pushing empty tubs on to

a creeper and I hated

it and hated all the

time I worked there for

six years I worked there

and hated it every minute

of it I developed more

muscles than what I thought

I had and very little

money

        joy came the day

I left to join the

army goodbye to Wingate pit

—————————

Out-bye on the engine plane

middle of the way round a curve

the hauling engineman put his brake on

suddenly

the tail rope jerked and

flew off the binding sheaves across

into the middle of the way and

caught him on the head

fracturing his skull

_____

15 hours out of the house every day I go to school at night
we're in school two hours   I hurt myself very sore to get
scholarship   I am ciphering and am at squaring dimensions
I read well   I sometimes read the History of England   sometimes I read the Bible   I write   I cannot say very well but I can
write

4

Large iron lamp full of burning coals through clouds of smoke
the engine-house and the massive framework around the shaft
with its ropes and pulley-wheels a few empty iron tubs and
stacks of timber ready for use in the foreground a row of coal-
wagons standing under the screens immediately behind

> *If I could do it I'd do no writing at all here. It would be*
> *photographs; the rest would be fragments of cloth, bits of*
> *cotton, lumps of earth, records of speech, pieces of wood and*
> *iron, phials of odors, plates of food and excrement.*
>
> (James Agee)

First task when he reports for work at midnight
collect a token he strings round his neck
identification in case of accident every day
three miners are killed (1939)
every day he collects his safety lamp his token

The shaft is a perpendicular drift, sometimes made semi-
elliptical at the mouth by means of boards; a few yards down it
becomes perfectly circular, from eight to ten feet in diameter.
It is cased by stone walling

for about eighteen fathoms down, or until the stone work can rest upon solid rock, when it is continued by being cut through the consolidated strata, and opens to the workings of the mine through strong arches.

Three raps: man riding
Two raps: start
One rap: stop.

When the chummens had taken the place of the fullens and the cage had been rapped away the winderman would lift the cage off the keps the banksman would pull a lever the cage was sent on its way.

Nobody puts his helmet light on
in the cage you'd
blind each other you
drop down in the dark

The only means of ascending or descending the shaft was in a kibble
    or loop
He came out of the workings to the shaft bottom and shouted
'Bend away to bank'
Swinging up the shaft the spring hook at the end of the rope caught
    an iron bunton which broke the hook and the loop and he dropped
    486 feet to the bottom

We go down two together

the loops have hooks are hooked into the link

one loop to two of us

one puts in his left leg and the other his right leg

and with our hands we cling to the chain

frequently others hang on like

sailors on a ship's rope

Above the top loop ten or twenty or more lads would catch the chain

till fathoms of rope and chain covered with human beings

dangled over the black pit at the Elvet pit two men

going down

a hook of another rope caught him by the hough

ripped off the skin of his leg like a stocking

the surgeon sewed up the leg but it all became dead flesh he

died five or six months after

———————————

Broomside Colliery
the cage left the surface with four men

stopped by the banksman's order
at the Low Main seam where
Isaac Rickerby was waiting

rapping the signal as he
passed some gear in he was
stepping into the cage as it
began to move down and
was crushed between the
cage and the shaft timbers

———————————

Xx xxxxxxx xx xxxx xxxxx, xxx xxx xxxxxxxx xxx xx xxx xxxxx xxxxx, xxx xxxxxxxx, xxx no light with him, attempted to get out of the cage, xxx did not see or forgot about the gate being closed, xxx ran his head against it and was knocked back into the shaft.
Xx xxx found on top of the other cage 75 feet below, xxx xxx xx xxxxxxxx xxxxxxx xxxx xx died on the following day

———————————

Thornley Colliery
attempting to cross a staple he
signalled the ascending cage away
started to cross at a diagonal and was
crushed by the descending cage

———————————

The cage had just come to bank, to the heapstead level,   a tub and
a tram in it   loaded with old timber,   He took the tub out, got
inside the cage, beside the timber tram, and told the winding
engineman to take the cage to the ground level;   fainted and
fell out, or attempted to get out of the cage before it stopped,
fell to the bottom of the shaft,   230 yards

———————————

At Haswell the shaft was 160 fathoms or 960 feet deep. The crab, a
sort of huge drum revolving horizontally, to which a rope was
attached, moved by a horse, was a very slow method of traction.
Some obstruction took place, and the corf, full of men, hung in the
shaft for an hour-and-a-half, exposed to a strong downward
current of air

it was 3 on a dark winter morning and nothing could be seen
Tak had!

5

inland shores in the pit   what the wavy floor was
and blue stone soft like when we were kids we used to write with
    at school
when it got wet it buried you like the houses on the Isle of White
    are sliding into the sea
in this band of stone are the fossils of the dinosaur we called it
    blos stone or mall

_____

Durham a dense tropical rainforest wide rivers flowing to the sea
flooding left thick layers of sand and mud on top of vegetable matter
    decomposed and compressed
in low-lying swamps peat then new layers of peat
process repeated over millions of years layer after layer of mudstone
    sandstone strata sequence of Westphalian coal measures bands
    of shale
steam coal house coal chinley coal gas coal claggy coal manufact-
    uring coal sea coal bunker coal pan coal crow coal sooty coal
    roondy coal coking coal cannel coal brown coal shaly coal parrot
    coal beany coal

_____

The coal measures of Northumberland and Durham occupy a triangular area of 900 square miles (including under-sea royalties), with its apex in the north near Alnwick and its base between Hartlepool in the south-east and Eggleston (near Middleton-in-Teesdale) in the south-west. Structurally, the field forms the western side of an irregular basin, elongated in a north and south direction, the eastern side of which is cut off by the sea. The seams outcrop on the west and south and some continue eastward beneath the North Sea. With the exception of a covering of Boulder Clay, the coal measures are exposed at the surface over the greater part of this area, being concealed beneath a cover of newer rocks in the south-eastern corner only.

―――――――――

Old workings and air-ways where nobody was working so quiet you could hear your own heart beating in the strata the forms of a leaf or a fish in the stone the iron quartz pyrites sparkling like gold

―――――――――

The roadway was 14 feet high
held up with arched girders

coalface around 30 inches high
but with 4 inches of steel top and bottom

you had 22 inches to crawl through
some coalfaces were 6 miles out
under the North Sea Bohemia's coast

Brian Muter

Well   you always   you had either a pricker or a stick and you
used to tap the top just to check   what the condition   the stone
was like   if it was   you used to get a nice ring if it was alright
if it was   you used to get like a holla sound if conditions were
poor and you'd shove props in as soon as you possibly could if
you had the holla sound

6

The darkness never changes. Seasons make no difference. Spring and summer, autumn and winter, morning, noon, and night, are all the same.

Coal and stone, stone and coal – above, around, beneath.

There is a path which no fowl knoweth, and which the vulture's eye hath not seen: The lion's whelps have not trodden it, nor the fierce lion passed by it.

(Job 28: 3, 7-8)

——————————

they rarely saw daylight for six months of the year

apart from Sundays the whole night's rest lasting till daylight

the one family dinner of the week

——————————

Pressing for more information, he inquired how long I had been down the pit.

'Seven years,' was the answer.

In most surprised tones he said, 'Have you not been up until now?'

I was surprised at him, and replied, 'Yes, every day except on rare occasions.'

'Why, I thought you pitmen lived down there always!'

John Wilson

———————

You do get
All sorts of temperatures
Down the mine sometimes
It's cold as winter sometimes
Hot as hell

———————

Youngest were the trappers of the barrow-way
where the putters pass they sit
in a hole like a chimney cut out in the coal

a string in their hand
all day in pitch black if the
candle went out or the oil ran out

noises of strata moving pieces of roof falling
rats mice scurrying round their feet
in muck and water cold and shivering

opening and closing heavy ventilation
doors for passing coal tubs
up to eighteen hours every day

Winter of 1844 we had neither, food, shoes, nor light in our first shift.

I was sent to mind two doors up an incline and the drivers flung coal and shouted to frighten me as they went to and fro with the horses and tubs.

yelling all day long
half naked
black
covered by sweat and foam

The wagon-man, Tommy Dixon, visited me, and cheered me on through the gloomy night; and when I wept for my mother, he sang that nice little hymn,

'In darkest shades if / Thou appear my dawning has begun'.

He also brought me some cake, and stuck a candle beside me.

    To reach the pit
    three miles from home
    on cold dark mornings
    sit crouching in a
    dark damp hole behind a door
    kicked and pushed
    here and there among
    lads and brutal men for
    twelve or thirteen hours
    was an experience I little dreamt of
    when we asked Neddy Corvey for
    work at the Leitch Colliery

10th November. – Xxxx Xxxxxxx, xx, a lad working xx Xxxxxx Xxxxxxxx, in the night shift, had stolen some gunpowder, and was taking it home with him in the early morning, xxx xxxxxx xxxxx in a piece of gas piping which he had thrust down his trouser leg to hide it xxxx xxxx, when a spark from the lamp hanging on his belt fell into the open end of the pipe

---

I became a door-keeper on the
barrow-way four years ago
up at four walked
to the pit by half-past
work at five no
candles allowed except my father
gave me four burnt about
five hours I sat in
darkness the rest of the
time I liked it very
badly it was like I
was transported I used to
sleep I couldn't keep my
eyes open the overman used
to bray us with the
yard wand he used to
leave marks I used to
be afraid the putters sometimes
thumped me for being asleep

—————————————

Near a door in the rolley way I held a string which pulled open
a door and which shut again of itself.

I could move about a little but must be on the watch to see if
anything was coming.

If I happened not to open the door in proper time I was likely
to get a cut of the whip.

Swarms of mice in the pit and I could sometimes take them by
a cut of the whip.

Midges sometimes put out the candle.
The pit is choke full of black clocks creeping all about.
Nasty things they never bit me.

—————————

I often caught mice.
I took a stick and split it and fixed the mouse's tail in it.
If I caught two or three I made them fight. They pull one
    another's noses off.
Sometimes I hung them with a horse's hair.
The mice are numerous in the pit. They get at your bait-bags
    and they get at the horse's corn.
Cats breed sometimes in the pit and the young ones grow up
    healthy.
Black clocks breed in the pit. I never meddled with them except
    I could put my foot on them.
A great many midges came about when I had a candle.

—————————

I used to come up at six
went home got dinner washed and went to bed.

no mischief in turnip or pea fields
in orchard or garden
but what I was
in it or
blamed for it

when the pits were idle I wandered

Houghton-le-Spring   Hetton   Lambton
Newbottle   Shiney Row
Philadelphia   Fence Houses   Colliery Row   Warden Haw
   Copthill

every wood dene pond and whin-cover
was known to us in our search for
blackberries mushrooms cat-haws crab-apples nuts

not a bird's nest in wall hedge or tree for miles around
escaped our vigilance

———————————

One day the overman sent us to a part of
the mine we'd never been before there was fire-damp

put out our candles one after another as fast as
we lighted them so we ran it was not safe

to try it on any longer and we began to
scramble our way back in the dark laughing we were

a great deal but we missed our way and got
into old workings abandoned for years and got lost we

wandered about for two whole days and nights and were
nigh starved to death afore we found our way out.

———————————

many who escaped to the higher workings
must have subsisted for some time on
candles horse-flesh and horse-beans

part of a dead horse was found near and
but few candles were left
though a considerable supply had been received
just before the accident

———————————

    Mushrooms
    grow in the pits
    at the bottom of the props
    and where the muck's fallen
    100 yards or more from the shaft

———————————

7

The stone fell about 160 feet,   the ascending cage was travelling
at 10 feet per second,   weight of the stone 63 lbs., the force of
impact, when it and the cage met, would be about
5½ tons.

_____

Herrington Colliery
cutting out a baulk with a saw on the engine plane
we set some timber
a stay from one side to the other to keep ourselves safe
the slip was not to be seen
before it fell without warning
no dribbling
just a fizzle and the stone came straight off he
died two days after

_____

piece of stone from a powder-shot
rebounded from the side of a tub and
hit a driver on the forehead
just above his left eye

_____

Burnhope Colliery he

finished his shift

ravelling out-bye

along a new travelling way

passing the upcast shaft

there was a door he opened

and stepped into the shaft

and fell

to the bottom

Xxx xxxxx xxxx xxx xxx xxxxxxxx xx xxx xxxxxxxxxxxxx xx xxx
xxxxxxxxx xxxxxxxx, xxx xxx engaged at a washing machine,
xxxxx xxx supplied with coals from a hopper. The coals had
stuck to the sides of this hopper, and were not running freely,
xxxx xxxxxxxx xxx xxxxxxx xxxxx xxxxxx, instead of using the
rod provided for the purpose, jumped into the hopper, xxxx xxx
xxxxxx xxxx xxxx xxxx xxxxx carried away down by the rush of
coals. Xxx xxxxxx xxxxx xxx xxxxxxxxxxx xxx xxx xxxxx, xxx
xxx xxxxxxxx, William Robinson, was beyond hope

---

until near midnight, when suddenly there was a rush of hot
water down the drift, which fell on   he was standing on
the scaffold in the sump, unable to get out, for two or three
minutes, and was badly scalded all over his body, dying after
15 days' suffering what coals sometimes cost

———————————

The engine took a set of ten waggons to the top of the incline

set away

a man on the back to brake them down he
saw a man walking on the track ahead

shouted and applied the brakes
and two men ran towards him shouting but

he was deaf the waggons hit him he
died the same afternoon

———————————

Struck by tram plate while using it as a lever   Fall of stone   Fall
down shaft from upper seam to bottom   Crushed by tubs on
horse-way   Fall of stone   Fall of stone fall of stone fall of stone
Head caught   against roof while driving   Fall of stone of stone
Crushed by tubs on engine plane   Struck on head   by horse
Crushed between wagons and wall   Fall of stone   Crushed by
tubs on engine plane   Crushed by tubs on engine plane
Crushed by the cage starting as   he was getting into it
Explosion of a shot   Run over by four tubs of stone   Head
crushed between tub   and timbers   Fall of stone   Fall of coal
and stone   Crushed on pulley wheel   Fall of stone   Fell into
sump and was drowned while changing cage chains   Run over by
trucks   Crushed between two trucks   Severely crushed knocked
down by and trampled on by his horse   Chain broke and the tub
ran back and   killed him   Crushed between wall and door by
passing tubs   Fall of

_____

      sounds of the
      gentle oozing of
      gas of water
      escaping from the close-grained coal around

_____

'It was supposed that George Stephenson and Sir H. Davy had discovered a true safety lamp. But, in truth, this very ingenious invention is like the compass that Sir Thomas More describes in his Utopia as given to a distant people. It gave them such confidence in navigation that they were 'farther from care than danger.' No lamp has been made, or, perhaps, can be made, that will prevent accidents when a feeder of gas is tapped, or a careless miner opens his lamp, or a drop of water cracks a heated glass, or a boy stumbles and breaks his lamp.'

(W. Stanley Jevons)

8

putting is sore work dragging the coal corves or tubs
using a harness called the 'soames'
a chain passed between the legs hooked to an iron ring
    attached to a
leather belt blisters as big as shillings and half-crown pieces
blisters of one day broken the next and the
girdle stuck to the wound crawling on hands and knees
dragging the coal through the tunnels from the workings to
the passages where pony putters could be used
dis thoo think we deserve to toil awl day in livin' tombs?

————————————

When I was putting I used to have an elastoplast the length of
my back on here   the scab would be catching the strut it was
that low   the seam was only 13 inches high in places just
about high enough to get a tub in   and you had to push it
in   bent like that   catching your back scabs on your back

————————————

Hangman to a murderer on the scaffold at Durham Gaol:
'You can have a reprieve if you start work, putting at the drift.'

Condemned man: 'Pull that lever.'

————————————

George Hancock

I was 15 year old and nine month
when I started to hand-putt
and that is the worst job God ever created
shoving it behind a tub
all day
it was horse's work
it was terrible conditions there was
nobody made
to have to do that
but of course it was there ...

and that was it

_____

for Ralph Hawkins

Smash me heart marra
me puttin's a' done after his
first day down the pit
head in his hands

he told his mother he
wished he was 65

9

Carbon monoxide is colourless odourless tasteless lighter than air

damps or foul airs kill insensibly

they are most in hot weather

infallible trial is by a dog and candles show it

in south winds colliers suffer from carbonic acid gas

white damp black damp and fire damp heavy sulphurous air not
    fit for breath

black damp or stink could knock a man down

————————————

Traces of gas in the dark

tiny little sparks in mid-air
or bubbling on the wet
black surfaces

————————————

Jim Green
I've seen fellas who were deaf
stone deaf underground
and they would
tap

sound of knuckles tapping a surface

the roof
and they would tell you
if
it's
safe

and if they said it wasn't safe you better take notice of them

because them seem to know something you didn't

———————————

and heard the blow, and see what it threw out of the pit, and shatter'd about the Gins: There was one thing very strange in it, as I was told, That a Youth of 15 or 16 Years of Age, was blown up the Pit and Shaft, and carried by the blast about 40 Yards from the shaft, the Corps was found all intire, save the back part of his head, which was cut off, though the Shaft is sixty Fathoms deep, which is an Argument of the mighty Force this Blast is of.
1705

———————————

Lumley Park the workmen worked on the vein of coal until they came to a cavity which was supposed had formerly been dug from some other pit but

on breaking of the hollow part the pent-up air got vent it blew up like 1,000 barrels of gunpowder and getting vent at the shaft of the pit burst out with such terrible noise as made the very earth tremble for miles around

nearly three score of people lost their lives in the pit and one or two who were at the bottom of the shaft, were blown quite out though sixty fathoms deep, and were found dead upon the ground.
1708

---

the lamp being let down at the request of the masons to rarefy the air in an instant took fire with a terrible explosion destroying men horses and all in its passage

noise of the explosion was heard above three miles around and the flash was visible as a flash of lightening

men below were drove by the force up the shaft or great tube like balls out of a cannon heads arms legs thrown out a great distance from the mouths of the pits the ground for acres was covered with timber coals etc.

Lampton Colliery near Chester-le-Street, 1766

---

50 or 60 yards away I heard a tremendous noise looked round
and saw the discharge come out of the pit-mouth like the
discharge of a cannon

it continued to blow I think for a quarter of an hour discharging
everything that had come into the current   stones came up and
trusses of hay

the ground all round the top of the pit was in a trembling state I
went as near as I durst go and everything appeared crackling
about me

The pit continued to blow every two or three hours for two days
some of the explosions equal to the first.
1806

———————————

Heworth morning of the 25th May 1812 about half past eleven
    darkness like early twilight
inverted cone of black dust carried away on a strong west wind
falling a continued shower a mile and a half around
covered the roads so thickly
footsteps of passengers were strongly imprinted in it

clothes, tobacco-boxes, shoes, the only indexes by which they
    could be recognised

bodies in ghastly confusion: some like mummies, scorched dry baked. One wanted its head, another an arm. The power of the fire was visible upon them all; but its effects were extremely various: some were almost torn to pieces, others as if they had sunk down overpowered with sleep. Some much burnt, but not much mangled. Others buried amongst a confused wreck of broken brattices, trapdoors, trams, and corves, with their legs broken, or their bodies otherwise miserably scorched and lacerated.

> From the position in which he was found
> as if he'd been asleep
> when the explosion happened
> and never after
> opened his eyes

———————————

William Bell working in the pit morning of the disaster
Hebburn 1849 he was knocked down and rendered deaf and
while he was making his way to the shaft he
fell and knew nothing until he found himself at home

———————————

we encountered two men one with a
light the other bearing something on his
shoulders a blackened mass a poor dead
burnt boy he was taking out a
little further on we found some waggons
turned bottom upwards and scattered in different
directions a horse lying dead directly in
the passage his head turned over his
shoulders as if in the falling he
had made a last effort to escape

It came like a heavy wind it blew all the candles out and small
coal about and it blew Richard Cooper down and the door upon
him.

———————————

As I knew many of the pitmen there at Haswell, I walked over
    to see their families.
In the Long Row every house save one had its dead.
In one house five coffins – two on the bed, two on the dresser,
    and one on the floor.

———————————

10

collieries idle or working short

time the foundry gone the township

one little part of the wreckage

hard times together

criss-crossing of kinship and friendship networks

little to do and nowhere to go

gas-lit main street

bare bones of existence abject poverty multitude of meanings

exploited sweated underpaid health ruined maimed

————————————

'I have to guard myself against waxing poetic on the theme of this great galaxy of villages each with the pit as its focal point, and each nurturing a sort of semi-tribal community which in the light of present-day urban society, seems almost a dream of paradise – a sort of pitman's Paradiso, safely set in the remote past. The corrective is to remember the harshness, the filth, the disease, above all the smells. At the same time, their achievements cry out for celebration. Against all the odds, they and the folk who inhabited them built up communities prepared for every contingency, little societies of great strength and resilience and full of vigour and humour.'

(Sid Chaplin)

———————

6th December 1934 I met a man
trudging under the rain along a

muddy road a mirror the
omniscient narrator he was

small sturdy perhaps forty-five his
unprotected clothes were wet

an empty pipe in his mouth
out of habit he said

no tobacco in his pocket aye
and no prospect of affording any

11

The horse he gets nothing to eat all day
but he wishes it

there's a well he drinks the water
comes down out of the coal

the horse knows me I like him

about five o'clock we put the rolleys at the side
take out the horses and
deliver them to the horse-keeper

if he be not there we
take off the harness
put them in the stable
give them hay and water

sometimes the horses are in a sweat
and we rub them down he
eats well all night

————————

a pony pulled a set of four or five tubs
several hundred yards
maybe in a shift raised 100 tubs
weighing around 75 tons
and walked six or seven miles

Dennis Fisher
first job I ever had
I was placed into the stables to work
I could have been a horse-keeper if I
wanted to I liked the ponies
liked working with the ponies
and without those ponies
and we had two hundred of them in Chilton colliery
there wouldn't have been
any coal production whatsoever
without the pit ponies
they were the ones that did all the work
taking the empty tubs in
to the coal-face for the coal-hewers
and bringing the full ones out
and it's not
it's not on the level
when you go down the mine it's not level
you're going up steep hills
and going down steep banks
it wasn't very easy work for the
pit ponies

Some people have a feast every pay-day

and some have spiced cakes and having spent

their money will live poor towards the end

of the fortnight for three or four days

or more until payday come again perhaps

they've only potatoes and salt for some days

—————————————

for Edmund Hardy

Occasionally the pit ponies
were brought out of the pit

and ran loose in two fields

again and again they ran

from one end to the other

—————————————

I have seen men working in the pit all day

with only a bottle of water

and oatmeal in it

———————————

Blackhall Colliery 1946 we had to run

quarter of a mile down the pit yard

to the netties

for 500 surface workers in shifts at various times

a plank of wood made for 4 persons to sit

no flush toilets them days

a fire hose

to wash all the excrement down a pipe

onto the Pit Dene

12

in 1914
a miner was severely injured every two hours
and killed every six hours
like a soldier remembering a campaign he said
the lads in the 'C' drift where I was
in there
there's only one left alive
all of them died young
Hank and all them
Hank collapsed and died
Wally   Purvis   Clemensey
all big hitters all gone

them's the empty chair in the club
and they all worked in the same flat

———————————

he'd been in the hewer's place six times and taken a full tub out each
    time
but he didn't come again so the hewer went out about 14 yards
found a pony and tub and shouted what's wrong
the pony moved the deceased fell out from between two props dead

there was no timber displaced
tub was on the way
pony standing quietly

———————————

The blue metal above the Low Main Post is five or six fathoms in thickness; it is loose and breaks away in small pieces.
Water runs down the side of the shafts and gets into the jacks, and slips, and loosens the stone. There are
41 fathoms of walling in this shaft   the place from which this stone fell,
xxxxx x xxxxxxxx xx xxx xxxx xxxxx xx xxx xxxxxxxx xxxxxxxx;
the stone is grey post, very close, and hard
and triangular in shape, xx xxx xx xxxxxx and came out above the water ring at the north-east side of the
shaft.

———————

Miners tell tales of disaster averted turning back any morning if they saw a black cat it was bad if they saw a black cat any morning they'd turn back

———————

flaming place that's safe in the pit?

Let the coal

Stay

There

13

the Friday night
there was a little laddie standing
at the pit gates
he asked a dark night he asked me
could he accompany me to Birtley
afraid of the dark you see
& I asked him who he was he says
I've left school today
Catholic school at Birtley
I've been to the colliery office
to get a job
he says me mother's a widow
and I can get a job at the pit
so the manager's told uz that I can
start on Monday
I says come on sonnie I says
you can go half way when I go
up Eighton Banks you can
go along to the huts where he was living in Birtley
canny little lad he was

so anyway I was chairman of the Lodge
and on the Tuesday following
never thought anymore about it
a man came from the pit to tell uz
that I had to go straight to the pit
there'd been a fatal accident

didn't know who it was
so off I went I
left me breakfast
and went to Bewick Main Pit
it's about a mile and a half or
two mile
here's this little lad
lying in the ambulance house
head off
top
been caught with the girder
he was killed outright
second day down the pit
at the Catholic school on Friday afternoon
and got his leaving certificate at fourteen
killed eh
nice state of affairs
and a widow to start with
from the first world war

14

Easington New Winning
influx of salt-water
specially number three shaft
rising and falling the
change of the tides

———————

Can you remember when we put a heading underneath
Whitburn?

Old Whitburn's North.

And they'd made a water standage. And we drove underneath
it, fired a shot and we were cleaning up, put the rings in. The
water started coming up like that. They had to gan and put
pipes in and draw all the water off.

That happened at Whitburn. If he had have fired that there
would have been hundreds of men killed.

When it did come away me and Jimmy were sitting in the tail
end getting wa bait. And Bob R. and Tommy C. was the
officials.

Could hear this bloody noise. Looked alang the face. And there's
coming alang ...

Within half an hour the whole Mullergit five hundred metres in was flooded completely. Reet alang the face, reet alang the tailgate.

And it took six weeks to pump down they found an underground lake and also stone archways which wasn't on the plans at all and they hadn't a clue where these archways came from. There was a swally in one of the gates. And you had to jump on the boat to get through the water.

---

       miners coming across the dunes
       every day come hail or rain or snow

       bent double into the wind sometimes
       they could hardly walk

       shadowy figures in the twilight

       they'd be soaking wet by the time they got to work
       and it was a wet pit
       soaking wet still when they got home

       not a bit of wonder they're all
       rheumatic bent old men now

       for all their strange appearance you knew
       no harm would come to you

Westoe was underneath the Permian there's a lot more water associated with the dykes at Westoe because of the proximity of the Permian, water bearing strata. This Permian, it didn't only stay in the one line, it intersected the seams. And the Permian's very wet.

_____

soaked knee-pads rubbing into the bones
wet straps cutting into skin

he used to come home soaking wet
this is before the baths were built
and we were always drying clothes in front of the
fire soaking wet they'd be
as if he'd been out in the rain

_____

Yell watta
day watta
red cankery poison watta

_____

Geordie used to hate wet workin.

And the day of his funeral, it was during the Strike. It was chuckin it down. We were at the gates of the cemetery, all wor badges on. And an aad couple came along. 'Huh. They're picketin the cimitiry noo, yer knaa. We cannot bury wor dead'.

And we followed the hearse up and Geordie's coffin was. Water actually came awer the top. It's a wonder he didn't wake up and yell. He hated water. He wouldn't get a wet note off Wilfy A.

15

In the Buddle Pit when the rope
broke or the cage left the conductors
all hands in the pit had to
seek their way to bank by an

old pit near Broomside we had to
travel and crawl through abandoned workings
broken-down roads blocked with old timber
falls of stone pools of water

puddles ankle deep and then ascend
on chain ladders amidst a stinking
stifling atmosphere of black damp
reaching Rainton bare-headed bruised and cut

———————————

We used to always have a saying
the lads at the end of the shift
you used to give a bit of a cough

and they used to say
gan on
get the blackuns up

mind it used to
be black   phlegm it was
just dust man

---

he came home took his shoe off   I could see the hole   he must
have broken bones in his foot   and he was wanting to go to work
the next day he said it would be all right

Sometimes I had misfortunes
such is my hands being lamed

and having my feet bad I
was also burnt by an explosion

it came upon me all at once
I had a candle to fill with

and I stooped down into a hole to fill
and the gas exploded I was

very much burnt
all about the body and also

on my legs where I
had no stockings

George Taylor

I learnt a lot off old miners

these old miners

they were old men

at forty-two years old

aa've had to gan with the owd bugger

and they were the nicest fellas in the world

and that's where I learnt the pit work

pit work

it's a hard trade

and every yard's a danger

It's a terrible thing, emphysema. When they give him stuff all coal dust came up.

Well he died of it, and my father died of that as well and he was first Bevin Boy in South Shields to say I'll not go down the pits. And they put him in Durham prison for six solid weeks for being defiant. It was in the *Gazette.* He was just eighteen years old.

And on the headlines it said 'YOUTH. I WILL NOT GO DOWN THE PITS'. Even his doctor who he was under, for bronchial, he wouldn't sign the certificate to give him to the man – what do you know, the judge or whatever.

All me mother knew – the policeman knocked at the door and he said: 'Can I have a toothbrush and a change of clothing'.

She says: 'What for?'

He says: 'Ralph's going straight up'.

He went to prison rather than go down the pit and when he'd finished his six weeks he was a changed young lad. And the day that he came out the feller knocked at me mother's door and said: 'Your Ralph has to report to Whitburn Colliery and start on Monday'. He made him go.

———————————

Ah man but aa was bad aa
nearly smelt brimstone that time

———————————

History the history of bodies in pain   impossible to button his
clothes lace his boots use a knife and fork hands are often
knocked skin abraded   local throbbing or 'beating'   pus will
track along the tendon sheaths most often to the back of the
hand   inflammation   considerable swelling in the centre of the
hand the skin will be hot and glazed   inflammation of the
synovial membrane of the wrist joint and of the tendon sheaths
swelling and thickening around the affected wrist-joint
stiffness of the joint pain on movement and crepitations   the
lesion may be erythematous   or may consist of boils the lower
part of the legs and the forearms round the ankles at the upper
level of the clog or boot and also round the waist at the level of
the waist-belt   coal dust is infected with staphylococci

—————————————

Tom Lamb
and me back was catching the roof
making scabs down yer back
called pitman's buttons

it would heal over the weekend
and you would go in and
knock them off on the Monday

—————————————

You had to work
because there was nothing else

gettin battered about
was part of the job

———————————

You'll have to cut the names out cos aa think he's still alive.

S. was a blacksmith at Cotia, and came out of his time there was
too many, so he took a job down the pit as a greaser, gannin'
round oilin' and greasin' all the machinery. And he was a very
funny lad, used to tek a set of claithes to the pit, after the
holidays, and the same claithes were there till the next holidays,
never used to change his work claithes. So they stunk. So did he.
And he had bad breath an'aall.

Anyway, we're aall in the cage. It was about '62, '63, when they
were starting to close the pits, and we were aall in the cage this
day, and we're crackin' on about that. They'd just shut that one
where the lad was supposed to have hit Robens, was it Lambton
D? It was just after that and we're coming up in the cage talkin'
about it, which one was next on the line.

We were in the top deck. Well the top deck has a bar runs across
it, and you can sort of lean on it, well S. was leaning on it. And
our Len says: 'Aye, aa knaa two bliddy mair they should shut'.
S says: 'Aye what's that?'
'Thy bliddy ARM pits.'

16

Air raid sirens were sounded after the Chamberlain
broadcast on the wireless which woke the baby all the
women of the pit streets used to hold beetle drives to raise
money for a victory party after England won the war.

———————————

Dennis Fisher

and each colliery was allotted a target
for tonnage
a tonnage target
and we were all patriotic
all the miners worked together to produce this target every
every week
and when we used to come out the pit on the Friday
the first thing we did
was look up at the pulley wheels
to see if the flag was flying
we had a union jack flying
we'd reached the target
we reached the target every week
till that flag
was flying in tatters

and then we got a new flag
in 1947 when the collieries was nationalised
and at last the pits belonged to us

so we thought

———————————

New Year's Day was Vesting Day
miners paraded the streets behind the lodge banner and colliery
band

to Brandon 'C' pit head
before a large crowd the blue flag was hoisted

N.C.B. in white in the centre
and a board fixed to the winding engine house:

'This colliery is now managed
   by the National Coal Board
      on behalf of the people.'

———————————

Geordie Ord

if this pit were to close
I'd accept me redundancy tomorrow

nearly 44 years down the pit
it's a fair good length of time

I haven't got the figures but
I know the people in Craghead
I would think about two or
three years after they're finished
retired at 65
nine out of every ten dies
simple reason is
their engine's finished
they've worked
that hard
all their lives

———————————

Count the shifts the
months the weeks days the hours minutes the seconds

———————————

just fancy
a man working 50 years down the mine
and he gets a piece of paper
a certificate (from the National Coal Board)
I'd have given 'em all a hundred pound
in fact some chaps doesn't come and even accept it
& I'm damn sure I wouldn't
and some hangs it up and put them in a frame

and some just throws it in the fire
and that's where mine would go

---

sometimes I wake up
and I've been thinking of the pit
as clear as crystal

some incident
however trivial it's
flashed back
in me mind
thirty-six year
down there you can't forget it
it's a lifetime it
was me life

Geordie Ord

everybody's brothers when they're down the pit
and that's the sort of thing I many a time sit
what's going to happen when the pits is finished
redundant
you haven't got that sort of comradeship
you just sort of
automatic drift apart

———————————

A man's bar they say they should have a man's bar
where you do what you want to do

I saw a woman in there one day in the bar
at Kelloe Club it was Robert Shutt's mother

and Harold Wilson jumps up straight on his feet
he shouts Mr. Secretary
there's a woman in the bar here mind

she says I'll not be a minute
I'll not be a minute and she sat down
telling somebody the tale but
she had to gan out

———————————

There's too many working people think they're middle class noo.

I can remember Jacky H. Can you remember Jacky H? At Westa.
I remember him. He used to flee all awer.

I used to say to him: 'Jacky why do you flee all awer? You're no
    better thought of, man'.
He says: 'I'm going to be colliery overman at this colliery and',
    he says, 'I don't care whose toes I stand on till I get there'.

Once he got the colliery overman's job that was a joke gan' round
    the pit. His lass went to the shop and asked for a pair of
    colliery overman's pit socks.

––––––––––––––

    Bill McKie
the were honest
and I can remember an occasion when
miners got paid
one shift of miners going down about half-past 9
got paid before the went down the pit
and the just put the money in the pocket
when they got down the pit
they hung their coat up
and I never heard of anybody losing one penny

––––––––––––––

Picking coal from

a waste heap

at Hebburn Colliery

he jumped onto

a moving wagon

full of coal

slipped

fell and

the wheels passed

over his neck

17

black crepe
hung on the pit banner at Durham Big Meeting
pitman's stoop
making your way in-bye on foot
breathing through dust
coming off like a black fog
driving the drift from the low seam
cutting coal with a windy pick

pneumoconiosis dermatitis nystagmus
bronchitis and emphysema
breathless wheezing and coughing

beat knee beat elbow torn or damaged knee cartilage
rheumatism hernias arthritis crutches empty jacket sleeves
his twisted frame in old age

black circles of coal dust round his eyes
small blue veins and blue-black
scars of coal dust cuts on his face

———————————

You'd see them
in the village struggling to
walk they
lost weight quickly

gaunt and thin
the club I drank in
used to call it 'Death Row'
ten miners sitting in a line

you saw it go from ten to nine
to eight to seven you can see
who were lucky
to be alive mind

but they can't get the words out
can't breathe properly
bent at right angles

———————————

Well I don't go out
I don't go out drinking or nowt
I can't get out any

I can't go out I can't go anywhere

even if I walk up the stairs I'm jiggered
and coming down I'm just as bad
I never dreamt I'd be like this and sometimes
you get days like
you're playing a tune you know like
and wheezing and
oh dear they say
we can hear you upstairs

when there was a club down here
I used to go down and have a drink now and again
but that was it
I couldn't dance or nowt I can't
bloody well walk never mind dance I'm
a bloody write-off here

waste of time really

18

Winter of 1810
    every pit was stopped
    without organisation or halls to meet in or strike pay or
    savings
    suffering from cold and hunger

delegates' meetings were hunted out by the owners and
    magistrates
mass meetings on the moors dispersed by troops

many arrests the Old Gaol and House of Correction at Durham
were so overcrowded some were held under armed guard in the
stables of the Bishop of Durham a Christian gentleman

families were evicted from their cottages and turned adrift in the
snow after seven weeks the terrible and savage pitmen starved
into submission

————————

        signing the bond
        indicating their assent and signature
        by stretching their hands
        over the shoulder of the agent
        touching the top of his pen
        while he was affixing the cross to their names

————————

I was at your hoose last neet
You are resisting not the oppression of your employers
And myed meself very comfortable
but the Will of your Maker
Ye hey nee family and yor just one man on the colliery I see ye've
a great lot of rooms and big cellars and plenty wine and beer in
them which I got me share on
the ordinance of that God who has said
Noo I naw some at wor colliery that has three or fower lads and
lasses and they live in one room not half as good as your cellar
that in the sweat of his face shall man eat bread
I don't pretend to naw very much but I naw there shudn't be that
much difference

---

workhouse closed to miners the terrible and savage pitmen village
after pit village thousands of families evicted their dwellings taken
by strangers families and furniture handed to their door

camped out on the moors on the roadside in ditches beneath
hedges and in fields under the open sky of the wet fag-end of
summer 1844 children the bedridden at Pelton Fell a blind
woman of 88 evicted out into the rain

throwing their household goods out into the road colliery carts
loaded with furniture moved away into the lanes formed the walls
of new dwellings tops covered with canvas or bedclothes

dozens prosecuted for trespass bound hand and foot forced onto treadmills to work off their fines

everywhere yeomanry militia dragoons regiments of foot troops of cavalry marines a strong force of London police

bright glitter of the huzzar's sabre point of the fusilier's bayonet

———————

1st August 1844. Two days ago the foundation stone of a monument was laid on Pensher Hill to the late Earl of Durham in the presence of 30,000 persons the cost exclusive of the stone which was given by the Marquis of Londonderry being £3,000. If the Marquis thought this noble deed should be recorded in history let it also be recorded that Henry Barrass was a working man and had worked in his pits for 30 years and that he is in his 80th year with his wife in her 75th and they have been turned out of their house.

———————

RESOLUTION: 'Seeing the present state of things and being compelled to retreat from the field through the overbearing cruelty of our employers, the suffering and misery of our families, and the treachery of those who have been their tools during the strike, we, at the present time, deem it advisable to make the best terms with our employers we can.'

_____

'If the workman is to be 'rudely handled' by natural laws, and stripped naked by the laws of political economy, he may some day be forced to seek for his protection outside of law altogether, and this is what all thoughtful men should seek to prevent. And let not the Owners forget themselves, history can repeat itself. Not hungry, but hungered men know no law, or are amenable to no reason, seeing that their famished state proclaims they have already past the boundary, where neither reason or humanity govern the affairs of life.'

(Durham Coal Trade Arbitration, 1876)

_____

Everybody followed Billy he used to call himself
a militant moderate
and to Billy it was a test of endurance
something we had to see through
like the Blitz
he wasn't going to go back
nobody was going back as far as Billy was concerned
we're gonna beat the bastards we'll
endure

it wasn't a political thing
it was a test of endurance

_____

after dark Dawdon women
crept near their pitheap
when your children are
cold they swarmed over the
coal even the bairns'
sand-buckets were filled

_____

We were on one side of the yard
and the miners were on the other
and Joe said come on I'll fight
the biggest of yours and I came out
I mean I drink with Joe in the club
and I backed him towards the wall
and I took off my helmet and coat
threw my cuffs and stick on the floor
and I put my fist up and said
come on Willis I'll have you any day
and he turned round and said
I'll not fight with you Stanger you
bought us a drink on Sunday

————————————

He was on strike on picket duty
I said well why you know it's
going to close down he said I
want a job for my son I
says do you want him to go
down the colliery I says my father
didn't want any of his boys to
go down he says it's a hard
it's the worst job you could ever

————————————

1

The miner demanded to know what law gave anybody the right
to stop him going home   he pointed at his blue uniform and
said this law   there were no photographers present

2

I used to have a drawing pin in my glove and I used to poke
them in the chest
that's enough from you you'd better behave
and the drawing pin used to stick in their chests and
they used to wonder what it was we can do all sorts of things
legality can be sorted out later

3

As you were driving past the pickets were shown fivers
and tenners at the windows brochures were waved at them there
were no photographers present
yeah there were them that waved fivers and tenners through the
window

———————————

three days police road blocks sealed the village off
nothing was allowed in
they stopped the buses at Easington Village
they wouldn't let any ordinary bus come down the main street
or through Horden
they had both ends of Easington Colliery blocked off
they were stopping searching all cars
people were ordered off buses

for three days police marched through the village

Gwent police   police from Northampton

I never thought I'd see scenes like this in Britain I never thought I'd

see what I've seen on the streets of Easington

we're occupied we've been occupied by the police

police some of them

wearing black

uniforms with no markings

———————————

'I stared at the monster, my head tilted back, and thought of all
the fine things that had been conjured out of it in its time: the
country houses and town houses, the drawing rooms and dining
rooms, the carriages and pairs, the trips to Paris, the silks and the
jewels, the peaches and iced puddings, the cigars and old brandies,
I thought I saw them all tumbling and streaming out...'

(J.B.Priestley, 1934)

———————————

Annual royalties accruing to landlords in the Northern Coalfields:

Ecclesiastical Commissioners	£370,000
Marquis of Bute (6 years average)	£155,772
Duke of Hamilton (10 years average)	£133,793
Lord Tredegar (6 years average)	£83,827
Duke of Northumberland (6 years average)	£82,450
Lord Dunravin (for 1918)	£64,370
Earl Ellesmere	£43,497
Earl Durham	£40,522

Evidence to the Coal Industry Commission, 1919.

————————

from Thornley Pit
low main best went to all the big houses in
London to the Palace
and Sandringham
I've seen tickets for the Palace

A' the hardship toils and tears
it gies to warm the shins o' London

————————

When Ellington closed in 1994 the world's press turned out to witness four ponies brought to bank for the last time and put out to pasture. Cameras and crews came from everywhere to present the event for television. Colin P., one of the pony handlers, was interviewed leading the last pony from the cage.

The day before five hundred men were made redundant in one of Europe's worst unemployment black spots and nobody else noticed.

19

I have a copy of *Proletarian Literature of the United States*, published by Martin Lawrence in London in 1935. It was given to me by an old Communist in Durham in January or February 1972. I think we met in the back seat of a car on the way to deliver hot soup and propaganda to a miner's picket line at a power station somewhere in the Team Valley. I think it was snowing. I'm sad and guilty that I no longer remember his name but I remember his strong lined face under his cap. He must have been over 70 years old. (I was 21 years old, an unemployed recent graduate). And I remember the story he told. Of waiting in the fields at night by the London to Edinburgh railway line during the 1926 General Strike. Bundles of the *Daily Worker* were thrown out of a passing express and spirited away by him and his comrades to be distributed among the striking locked-out pitmen in the area. I knew the spot: a triangle of ground between Low Flatts Road, the main railway line and another line that crossed over taking Swedish iron ore from Tyne Dock up to the steel works at Consett. I'd sometimes played there as a child when there were still pitmen on the windy fells west of Chester-le-Street. There are none now. But I don't know how the book came into my hands. I'm not sure I ever met him again. I think it got to me via somebody else, with a message. There is nothing written inside the book. But I think I still know what the message was. I don't know the words, though I imagine I do, across those gaps of time. Forty years; and eighty-seven years, since the great lock-out of 1926. The book's cover is faded green, the spine is frayed and hanging off. Its 384 pages include the writing of none of the leftist American poets active in the 1930s whose work was then inspiring me – George Oppen, Charles Reznikoff, Lorine Neidecker, Louis Zukofsky. And looking again through its yellowing pages on a grey autumn afternoon in 2013, there are few of its contributors I have ever read with any great interest –Kenneth Fearing yes, and perhaps Kenneth Patchen and Muriel Rukeyser. But I have taken this book with me to every place I have lived since 1972 – seven addresses, which doesn't seem very many, and the last three in London, a long way from the Lambton Worm and Low Flatts Road and the little bridge over the railway line that still heads from King's Cross north to Newcastle, or from Newcastle south.

20

Category D: Those from which a considerable loss of population may be expected. In these cases it is felt that there should be no further investment of capital on any considerable scale, and that any proposal to invest capital should be carefully examined. This generally means that when the existing houses become uninhabitable they should be replaced elsewhere, and that any expenditure on facilities and services in these communities which would involve public money should be limited to conform to what appears to be the possible future life of existing property in the community.

———————————

the house where I was born
number 21 Lower King Street
early 60's we realised
something was going to happen
which was the
knocking down of the Lower Street houses

so we decided to
look for higher ground
we found a house up in High Thompson Street
not only had it the luxury of gas it also
had the luxury of electricity
which we'd never ever had
chance to get a television

in 1969
we got the compulsory purchase order
that we had to go the inevitable
to 'the reservation'
had happened

————————————

I nearly broke me heart an'all
cos I love Witton Park
and I belong Witton Park
me heart's Witton Park
and I lived in Witton Park all me life
and I never took no hurt in it

————————————

But for instance
there's a lady gone out of that street there
74 years of age
she was bred and born in that house
she's never moved in her life and
she's being moved on the new estate so

how do ye think she takes to it?

————————————

Ivy Gardner's photographs
All these things
are my life

this one
was when they took the colliery down
that was me gran's street
that's the school

that was when me gran's house was knocked down

_____

This little village here
it was a thriving Roman village when London was a
grazing ground for Roman donkeys

_____

'The villages were built overnight – the Americans are much
more realistic about mining than we are. They know it's a
short-lived thing, relatively speaking. Even if there is fifty years
of coal – what's fifty years? So they talk about mining camps,
we talk about villages, which   is one of the oldest words in the
language. It means a permanent settlement. But most of the
Durham villages were, in fact, camps, and they were put down
as camps.'

(Sid Chaplin)

_____

Very strange seeing the remaining walls wall-paper sometimes peeling off to be able to see the allotments through the gaps all the rubble lying about it looked like a scene from the war.

Waterhouses   in a wood   kerbstones

21

Men would put their lamps face down in the dust and say, 'I mind once ...'

And you'd get a story.

_____

If they had little time, they had less inclination to be examined, and still less to answer the questions of a total stranger; and even when their attention was obtained, the barriers to our intercourse were formidable. In fact, their numerous mining technicalities, northern provincialisms, peculiar intonations and accents, and rapid and indistinct utterances, rendered it essential for me, an interpreter being inadmissible, to devote myself to the study of these peculiarities ere I could translate and write ... Even where evidence could at last be elicited from them, it was so intermingled with extraneous remarks, explanatory of their opinions upon politics and public and private affairs, foreign to the question addressed to them, that it was essential that a large portion of it should be 'laid out' by a process analogous to their own 'separation'.

_____

Get those miners who can tell the brilliant stories and sit them down and get them to tell the stories from the stories you make something to house the stories something that's right now that will be able to be listened to and appreciated well beyond their lifetime something like a vocal archive that could be listened to people and appreciated time after might be another way to do a commemoration plenty of miners still live here

———————————

       To record them and make a record
       as a monument
       is more of a monument

       instead of a sculpture
       the stories themselves

       all those stories you heard
       when you were young
       go   there's no record

———————————

In Durham Cathedral a miner's lamp is kept lit each day a page is turned in the book of remembrance colliery by colliery the names of men and boys who died underground with their ages and dates of their death marks of identity about which no man had any say and each man has no say.

22

From Ric Caddel's Back Kitchen Window

Mile after mile the wet roads the weak light
Empty streets
In plenitude of nature
Windswept
In freezing rain in silence that
Familiar place
Dark hills huge clouds blank
Stone on these slopes the same
End from any source

A thousand stratagems

Vanishing into the air

Ego

Scriptor

[1981]

Ric was uneasy about the title of this poem I remember. He wouldn't come out and say so directly, of course. But I could sense some reserve. The fact was, that from the back of Cross View Terrace you could see a mile or so across to Langley Moor, a pit village where my grandfather was a pitman for most of his life and where I spent a good deal of time as a child. Ric and I walked down that long steep hill a couple of times but we never got as far as Langley Moor. A pub always intervened. By 1981, when I drafted this poem, Ralph Seed had been dead for a decade. And the world of my childhood seemed long gone. So it was a poem about death and about the disappearance of the past (and of the poet). And it was evoked by that particular wintry landscape on an actual January day when I looked out of that particular window. I also liked the several connotations of the name 'Cross View'. Now the death of Ric, who I knew for 30 years, forces me to read this poem in a different way. The words on the page are the same. But it is now a different poem.

London 23 April 2003

This is to remember Ric Caddel – and now Bill Griffiths too:

> Byker Hill and Walker shore
> Collier lads for evermore!
> Pit-laddie keel-laddie
> Cold salt
> Waters of the Tyne
> Autumn waters of the
> Tyne golden
> Shadows in the last rays smoking
> Till howdy-maw

23

forgotten spaces organized amnesia the activity of coal mining
erased beneath the surface of the visible rising mine-waters
entrail acidic salts they saturate voids

Romans left more traces in Durham County than the collieries
by the end of the twentieth century few traces of their
existence nothing commemorates places where several
generations thousands worked

and dozens sometimes hundreds died the sense of emptiness
experienced in a place which is losing its memory how to
know a place or represent something you can't see that isn't
there everything I don't remember

we treat what is
as inevitable   we stand on the ground of accomplished fact
everything that is but

how did the accomplished fact become one become 'is'

———————————

That's all over County Durham though, isn't it.

There's not many winding gears left.

They're all planted into little hills all over Durham.

Thirteen-fifty level – and they sent us down for to drive further in. And we went about a mile and a half in and the coal seam was about six foot six high, all coal, beautiful coal! And that was the reserves of coal. That was the reserves of coal that they could of had. And it was about six foot six, all good coal, beautiful coal. And they just left it.

24

      coal dust it
      settled on everything
      between the smallest cracks
      wedges that
      pried apart the world

―――――――――

Place rather than dates events rolling upland low ridges valleys with a strong east-west grain. Memories of others ancestral beings gently rounded ridges occasional steeper bluffs. Frozen for ever at a particular moment they sat down and became a part of the place for ever they turned into the place.

Not for ever   for as long as

as anyone remembers then
drift off without leaving

any residue

'We'   like smoke over the fields like rain

Fragments of heathland survive on infertile acidic soils.

In the beginning they went onto the spoil heaps picking out the coal until there was no coal left then down in Bloemfontein woods they cleared the soil away and they started working this seam so we had fires during the 1926 lockout.

Ancient oak woods in steep-sided denes on the banks of rivers and streams an asymmetry the landscape a waxing gibbous moon   high in the east at sunset the owl of Minerva

takes flight   only as night falls

_____

Everything that was lived
experience has
moved away
into

heritage reclamation landscape

blocked drift-mouths ramps collapsed tunnels disused railway
lines viaducts old coke
ovens spoil heaps slurry lagoons

new grassy fields smooth green slopes not quite
real among rolling upland ridges and valleys

dry stone walls thorn hedge
straight enclosure roads

immediacies of an ordinary afternoon where
something happened

times of the southern dynasties where strikes and closures it
was
always ganna gan

———————————

oscillate on a semi-tone hear both notes at once a chord
unresolved or archaeology the notion of strata lines edges
blurring edges   discontinuity where/when one layer becomes
another each residual layer containing information

fragments left from human occupation   left in a midden
    sludge dregs the lees

———————————

The true coal formation consists principally of extensive parallel
strata of coal, covered by strata of shale, containing impressions
of vegetables, and not unfrequently remains of freshwater shell
fish and animals.

The strata are frequently intersected by cracks or breaks, which
are filled with gravel or sandstone, and sometimes with a sink
or bending, locally denominated troubles.

25

Kimblesworth   Waterhouses   Witton   Wham

       Pelaw   Pelton   Stargate   Plain

Toronto   Hobson   Phoenix Drift

       Lambton   Waldridge   Tudhoe Mill

Quaking Houses   Langley Moor

       Randolph Hutton   Tanfield Lea

Brancepeth   Cragheed   Clara Vale

       Lumley   Harraton   Chester Moor

Chopwell   Cornsay   No.1

       Wingate   Ushaw   Herrington   Esh

Shildon   Beamish   Sacriston   Lintz

       Blackhall   Edmondsley   Framwellgate

Handen Hold   Trimdon Grange   Wheatley Hill

       Dragonville   Hamsteels   Dean and Chapter

Eden   Brandon   Pity Me

_____

'Nana and grandad's at Langley Moor'
the place was called

from Chester the 42 for Crook
off at the Boyne up Front Street
on the left past Brandon Lane

can't remember the number

listening you
cannot see how it was

pictures photographs shadows
changing on the wall

tangle of time frames unpainted
sunlight   and it's still there yes

a Saturday morning

a few thousand Saturdays ago

Notes

Thanks are due to the editors of *Intercapillary Space* (2014) and *Snow* 3 (2015), where some sections of this poem were first published. Parts of section 22 were published in 'In Memoriam Richard Caddel, 13 July 1949–1 April 2003', *Jacket Magazine*, no.22 (May 2003). The poem had previously been printed in John Seed, *History Labour Night*, published by Ric Caddel's Pig Press in Durham in 1984.

Page vi   'Workings in a Mine', J.H.H. Holmes, *A Treatise on the Coal Mines of Durham and Northumberland…* (1816)

Page 13   Bill Griffiths, *Pitmatic: The Talk of the North East Coalfield* (Newcastle-upon-Tyne, 2007), p.51

Page 24   James Agee and Walker Evans, *Let Us Now Praise Famous Men. Three Tenant Families* (new edition, Boston 1988), p. 13.

Page 33   John Wilson, *Memories of a Labour Leader: The Autobiography of John Wilson, J.P., M.P.* (London, 1910), p. 95.

Page 44   W. Stanley Jevons, *The Coal Question* (2nd ed., 1866), p.65.

Page 54   Sid Chaplin, 'Durham Mining Villages,' *Mining and Social Change. Durham County in the Twentieth Century*, edited by Martin Bulmer (London, 1978), p. 70.

Page 86   *Durham Coal Trade Arbitration: February, 1876* (Durham 1876), pp. 30-1.

Page 90   J.B. Priestley, *English journey: being a rambling but truthful account of what one man saw ... during the autumn of the year 1933* (new edition, London, 1987), p. 337.

Page 95   *County Development Plan* (Durham, 1951), pp. 77-78.

Page 97   Sid Chaplin, 'Durham Mining Villages' p. 63.

Page 99   *Commission of Enquiry into the Employment of Children in Mines*, 1842.

Postface

I've never been down the pit. My grandfather Ralph Seed – pronounced Rarf – worked down the pit around Brandon and Langley Moor for most of his life. So did his eldest son, uncle Jim. I remember him telling me how he left school on the Friday afternoon and some pit manager said to his dad, 'your lad'll be starting on Monday?' And he did. My father was marched off to Germany at the end of the war and avoided the pit. His mother, my grandmother, Evelyn Nolan, was from several generations of mining stock too. I found her brother, Cornelius (Con) Nolan, listed as an accident victim at Bowburn colliery in 1940. I think I remember Uncle Con's amazing curly eyebrows and his wiry frame and deep voice (some 20 years later) – or was that Uncle Henry? My other grandfather, my mother's father, was too damaged by his experiences in the First World War trenches, which got him the Military Medal and chronic bronchitis, to work down the pit. But his father John Carroll was a pitman. So was his father in turn, also called John Carroll, who had escaped from Ireland as a child in the 1840s. He was a pitman around Wigan in the 1860s and 1870s and later around Durham. My last sighting of him is in the 1901 census, listed as a retired hewer and widower, living with his daughter Margaret (Moore) and her husband in the little pit village of Kimblesworth. I do not remember his son, my great-grandfather John Carroll. I was two when he died, in his early 90s, but my mother told me several times how he'd held my hands to help me to walk as a stubborn impatient toddler. I think it was through him that I was called John.

So for what it's worth, I can claim several generations of Durham coal-mining stock on both my father's and my mother's side, as of course can hundreds of thousands of others today, scattered around the globe. And coalmining was a major part of the environment in which I was brought up in the 1950s and 60s around Chester-le-Street. Fathers of school-friends were pitmen, including Jock Purdon and Joe Donnelly. And my wife's father, John McTaff, was a Durham pitman too. But all this is by-the-by. You don't need to be of coal-mining stock or to have worked down the pit or live in Durham County to write about Durham and coalmining. These do not necessarily qualify you; nor does their absence necessarily disqualify you.

And this isn't biography, auto- or otherwise. What I have done in this piece of writing is to trawl through hundreds and maybe thousands of pages of printed sources – books, parliamentary reports, newspapers, magazines. I've also worked on source materials via many websites. I've been particularly keen to *listen* to the voices of miners – and their families – and so I've transcribed bits of recorded interviews for radio and television, some going back as far as the 1960s. From all this material, a tiny fraction of what is available about the Durham coalfield and its workforce, I have selected bits and pieces that attracted my attention. I had no plan, no idea of what I was looking for, though obviously my selections were partly determined by preconceptions – some conscious, some unconscious. I then cut, rewrote and spliced this material together in various forms – prose, verse of various kinds, with punctuation, without punctuation, arranged on the page in various ways. And with no outline or narrative or theme in my mind I shuffled and reshuffled this material: ellipsis, juxtaposition, disjunction, parataxis, fragmentation...

I was conscious that my pursuit of material here was not the same as a historian's. I was reading in a more haphazard (and un-disciplined) manner. My focus was wider. My attention was different. A more striking difference was that I sometimes rewrote my sources and interjected material of my own. This is a mortal sin for the disciplined historian who has to treat sources as sacrosanct. It's like doctoring evidence in a court of law or lying in the witness box. In my case, I was not revising my sources to fit a thesis since I had no thesis. I was merely interested in making the writing sharper, crisper, more precise, or at least more interesting. Or perhaps I was just enjoying cutting and pasting, like a child sitting on the floor brandishing shiny scissors surrounded by scraps of bright paper. Having said that, I did treat my sources with respect and I have invented nothing. (*Note to librarian*: please do not shelve in the 'Fiction' section.) I was particularly keen to respect the language of my oral sources and in places the writing follows exactly, or as exactly as I can hear, the pauses and incoherence of the speaking voice – though sometimes it doesn't. And where I could I have usually identified the speaker, as found in the source I'd used. Serious works of history provide a bibliography precisely so that other historians can examine these sources, check for misuse or selective use of evidence. There was no scholarly rationale for doing this here, but I have listed below a few sources I have used.

It is almost half a century since Hayden White criticised historians for turning their backs on the literary innovations of modernism.

'There have been no significant attempts at surrealistic, expressionistic, or existentialist historiography in this century (except by novelists and poets themselves) … It is almost as if historians believed that the sole possible form of historical narration was that used in the English novel as it had developed by the late nineteenth century.' ('The Burden of History' (1966), in Hayden White, *Tropics of Discourse: Essays in Cultural Criticism*, (Johns Hopkins University Press, Baltimore, 1978), pp. 43-4.)

Despite one or two exceptions in recent decades, the charge is still probably fair. One major exception is provided by Walter Benjamin and if there is one historical work that *Brandon*

Pithouse has some elective affinity to, it is his *Arcades Project*, his massive unfinished historical assemblage of materials from nineteenth-century Paris.

> 'The first stage in this undertaking will be to carry the principle of montage into history. That is, to assemble large-scale constructions out of the smallest and most precisely cut components. Indeed, to discover in the analysis of the small individual moment the crystal of the total event.' (Walter Benjamin, *The Arcades Project*, translated by H. Eiland and K. McLaughlin, (Cambridge, Mass., 1999), p.931.)

Had I world enough and time I would write at greater length about Benjamin's work, about its resistance to the conventional historian's strategy of scholarly inventory and interpretation, about its use of montage – and about the powerful creative matrix out of which it emerged in the 1920s, a matrix that included Cubism and Surrealism, the film theory and practice of Eisenstein and Vertov, Kafka and Proust, James Joyce's *Ulysses*, and Georg Lukacs's *History and Class Consciousness*.

Brandon Pithouse doesn't claim the status of 'History'. But nor, on the other hand, does it aspire to 'Poetry' – the territory of other great and jealous powers. It is not a long poem nor is it a collection of poems. It is an *investigation* of what can be done with source materials. It asks questions of the reader. Some sections have punctuation, some don't. Some are clear and straightforward pieces of prose broken up into lines or fairly conventional free-verse forms. There is much use of oral testimony which is represented in lines. Others are different in style. I wanted to keep moving, challenging myself and the reader to ask — what are these patterns on this white surface, how do I make sense of them? And yet the content is generally clear and made up of contemporary eye-witness accounts and real events. The formal presentation is meant to draw attention to itself as words on paper – but at the same time it is not trying to 'aestheticise' painful realities, nor distort for trivial literary purposes the voices and the experiences of real people. Something of the cold light of the real, of specificity and contingency, of the pain of physical labour and the suffering of real people, – 'the cruel radiance of what is', James Agee called it – filters through these texts I hope. When I trim down some testimony and then break it up into lines I see (and hear) things I hadn't seen (or heard) before. Maybe an open-minded reader can too? I discussed some of these questions in the 'Afterword' to John Seed, *Manchester: August 16th & 17th 1819*, (Intercapillary Editions, London 2013).

Despite exalted notions of the author, writers work with the materials they find around them and try to hammer out some kind of new thing with bits of discursive wood lying around and rusty nails and old string and glue. What I am doing here might even be compared to a film-maker creating a documentary out of other people's bits of film and sound recordings, interspersed with some slight commentary. Editing as creative act! And this makes me think of another great unfinished project: Eisenstein's film of Marx's *Capital*, a project stimulated by his reading of Joyce's *Ulysses* at the end of the 1920s. See also Alexander Kluge's monumental 9-hour film: *News from Ideological Antiquity: Marx/Eisenstein/Capital* (2008). So perhaps *Brandon Pithouse* is really a set of notes for a film that can never be made – and a footnote to Chapter 10 of Volume 1 of Marx's *Capital*.

History? Poetry? Film script even? In the end these questions don't matter very much, though they could take us along interesting detours on a dull afternoon. Perhaps I could just say that when Ezra Pound's *Cantos*, William Carlos Williams' *Paterson*, Charles Olson's *Maximus Poems* and Charles Reznikoff's *Testimony* collided with Walter Benjamin's *Arcades Project* and the first volume of Marx's *Capital* and the newly-published *History and Class Consciousness* of Georg Lukacs, in pubs and CIU clubs around Durham in the early 1970s this was what resulted – though it took another forty years to gather up some of the pieces and try to put them together.

Sources

Two valuable sources for listening to miners are 'Man in his Place: Durham: A Man's Life, 1', Broadcast BBC 1 (1972); http://www.beamish. org.uk/mining-life and 'Planning for Destruction: the D-villages of County Durham', a programme by Caroline Beck, broadcast BBC Radio 4, 1 September 2008: http://www.bbc.co.uk/programmes/b00bbnxr

Five wonderful websites for anybody interested in the Durham coalfield:

Reports on mining disasters: Durham Mining Museum: http://www.dmm. org.uk/names/index_17.htm

Database of Coalmining Accidents and Deaths: Coalmining History Resource Centre: http://www.cmhrc.co.uk/site/disasters/index.html

The Durham County Record Office database of Durham collieries: http:// www.durhamrecordoffice.org.uk/Pages/DurhamCollieries.aspx

Durham in Time, Durham Miner Project: http://www.durhamintime. org.uk/durham_miner/index.htm

The Tommy Armstrong Society: http://www.pitmanpoet.org.uk/Welcome/ welcome.htm

I have consulted several invaluable M.A. and Ph.D theses and I'm grateful to their authors:

Atkin, Michael (2001) *The 1984/85 Miners strike in East Durham, A study in contemporary history*, Ph.D, Durham University. Durham E-Theses Online: http://etheses.dur.ac.uk/2015/

Bunn, Leanne, (2010), *Changing Landscapes: Norman Cornish and North East Regional Identity*, Ph.D, University of Northumbria, Newcastle-upon-Tyne.

Doyle, Aidan (2001), *The Colliery Aesthetic: cultural responses at the end of industry*, Ph.D, Durham University. Durham E-Theses Online: http://etheses.dur.ac.uk/4275/

Emery, Norman (1984), *Pease and Partners and the Deerness Valley: aspects of the social and economic history of Waterhouses, Esh Winning and Ushaw Moor*, M.A., Durham University. Durham E-Theses Online: http://etheses. dur.ac.uk/7831/

McIntyre, Mary Patricia (1992), *The Response to the 1984-85 Miners' Strike in Durham County: women, the Labour Party and community*, Ph.D., Durham University. Durham E-Theses Online: http://etheses.dur.ac.uk/3462/

As to printed volumes, I've dipped into far too many to list here, including Parliamentary Papers, periodicals and newspapers. I list the following merely as useful places to start reading.

Benjamin, Walter, *The Arcades Project*, translated by H. Eiland and K. McLaughlin (Cambridge, Mass., 1999).

Bulmer, M., ed., *Mining and Social Change: Durham County in the Twentieth Century* (1978).

Colls, Robert, *The Pitmen of the Northern Coalfield: Work, Culture and Protest, 1790-1850* (1987).

Crookston, Peter, *The Pitmen's Requiem* (Newcastle-upon-Tyne, 2010).

Eisenstein, Sergei, *The Film Sense*, edited and translated by Jay Leyda (New York, 1957).

Goldsmith, Kenneth, *Uncreative Writing. Managing Language in the Digital Age* (New York, 2011)

Griffiths, Bill, *Pitmatic The Talk of the North East Coalfield* (Newcastle-upon-Tyne, 2007).

Hudson, Mark, *Coming Back Brockens. A Year in a Mining Village* (1994).

McIvor, Arthur and Ronald Johnston, *Miners' Lung. A History of Dust Disease in British Coalmining* (Aldershot, 2007).

Marx, Karl, *Capital: A Critique of Political Economy*, Vol.1, translated by Ben Fowkes (1976).

Milne, Seumas, *The Enemy Within: The Secret War Against the Miners* (30th anniversary edition, 2014).

Moran, Laurie, *The History of Brandon Colliery 1856-1960* (Durham, 1988).

Portelli, Alessandro, *They Say in Harlan County: An Oral History* (Oxford, 2011).